THE
METHOD

Cover image   ©The owner of the Archimedes Palimpsest

Collage timeline created by   Sasha Steensen
and produced by   Drew Nolte

Book design by   Colie Collen & Rebecca Wolff

Published in the United States by   Fence Books, Science Library 320, University at
Albany, 1400 Washington Avenue, Albany, NY 12222, www.fenceportal.org

Fence Books are distributed by   University Press of New England
                                                            www.upne.com

and printed in Canada by   Westcan Printing Group
                                                            www.westcanpg.com

Library of Congress Cataloguing in Publication Data
        Steensen, Sasha [1974–]
        The Method/ Sasha Steensen

Library of Congress Control Number: 2008934253

ISBN 1-934200-17-4
ISBN 13: 978-1-934200-17-9

FIRST EDITION

FENCE BOOKS are published in partnership with the University at Albany and the New York State Writers Institute, and with help from the New York State Council on the Arts and the National Endowment for the Arts.

THE AUTHOR wishes to thank the editors of the following publications, in which some of these poems (or versions thereof) first appeared: mid)rib, Little Red Leaves, Shiny, La Petite Zine, Goodfoot, Fence, Denver Quarterly, and Slope. Thank you to Rebecca Wolff and Catherine Wagner for including "The Stranger at the Gates" and "I Hear America Swimming" in the anthology Not For Mothers Only: Contemporary Poems on Child-Getting and Child-Rearing (Fence 2007). The Future of an Illusion was published as a chapbook by Dos Press; a sincere thanks to Julia Drescher and Chris Martin.

Deepest gratitude is extended to Matthew Cooperman, Gordon Hadfield, and Rebecca Wolff for their careful and considerate readings and to Murat and Nina Ergin for graciously housing me in Istanbul as I tracked The Method's paths.

THE
METHOD

SASHA
STEENSEN

FENCE BOOKS
ALBANY, NEW YORK

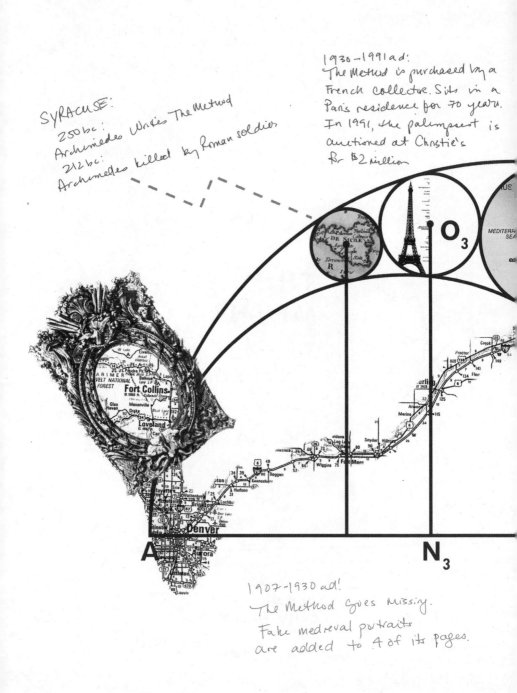

SYRACUSE:
250 bc:
Archimedes Writes The Method
212 bc:
Archimedes killed by Roman soldiers

1930-1991 ad:
The Method is purchased by a
French collector. Sits in a
Paris residence for 70 years.
In 1991, the palimpsest is
auctioned at Christie's
for $2 million

O_3

A N_3

1907-1930 ad:
The Method goes missing.
Fake medieval portraits
are added to 4 of its pages.

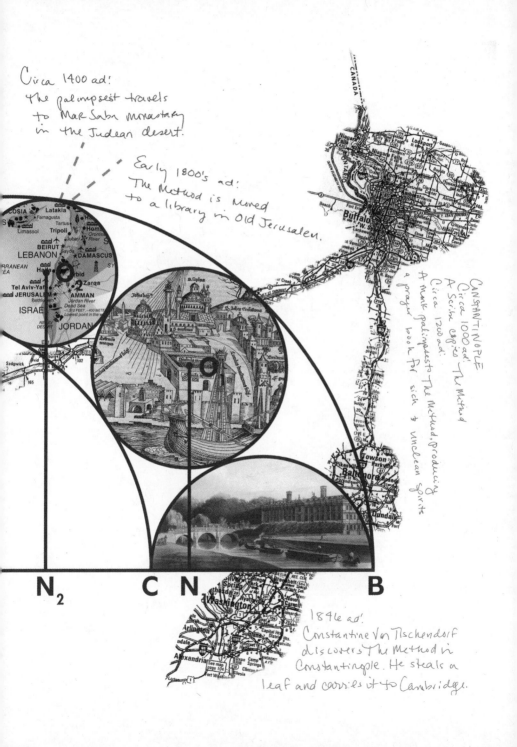

Circa 1400 ad:
The palimpsest travels
to Mar Saba monastery
in the Judean desert.

Early 1800's ad:
The Method is Moved
to a library in Old Jerusalem.

CONSTANTINOPLE
Circa 1000 ad:
A Scribe copies The Method

Circa 1200 ad:
A monk palimpsests The Method producing
a prayer book for sick & unclean spirits

N₂   C N   B

1846 ad:
Constantine Von Tischendorf
discovers The Method in
Constantinople. He steals a
leaf and carries it to Cambridge.

for Gordon and Phoebe,
fellow trespassers at St. John Studios

CONTENTS

road, come pass
with me terrors
by the side
of seas & easterlies

She dug the box
out of the closet.
She stuffed the baby's clothes
with rags
until a body
like a scarecrow's
filled the clothes.
She placed the body
in the bed
beside her.

MORROW-HEARTED METHOD DREAMS

Every little whale-thought waits
awhile, then dives deeper
into sleep.

Once awake, blowing hard
for air, The Method dunno
what he saw
there.

Ganging to remember
how he ate stars
how his liver escaped out his anus
and the sun rose through his genitals

or, how his eyebrows,
        the two parents, or two sons, or two partners, or two spouses
        or two handmaids, or two proxies
became bushy and beautiful, then fell out.

Only now,
beached on the Cape,
driftwood stuck and nudged
into each side
by curious vacationers
does he know how every object
that looks like an object
will be destroyed
finally.

AFTER CENTURIES OF MISTREATMENT

Each angle Archimedes draws

ends up in an orphanage
where it is stolen at night

and scattered.

Like a good son before he becomes bitter,
The Method lets Archimedes linger.

It's like having Archimedes's brain in a box,
pushing his way

past security
ticker, cutter,

Method in hand,
hand in air, as the plane

creeps
past us,
papyrus,
you
little
coward.

IN MOMENTS OF GRIEF, THE METHOD RECOLLECTS

Imaging a shadow-show in an inverted bowl
his doric dialect illuminated by candlelight:
bowl, sky; candlelight, sun
a phenomena, a phenomena, a phenomena.

Can the concept of a holy war belong to a century, he wonders
do roads, by their very existence, express conditions of political power,
    he wonders
used to be, he remembers, one could go by good road from York to
    Constantinople
in b.c. even, in six weeks even

or his holidays on the coastal ring road of Sicily, on the beach
under the bougainvillea, where he gave rim jobs
to his maker till he cried "Eureka! Eureka!" and died.

Around the ring road, and back to Syracuse, a body, a body, a body
buried under the briars and forgotten until
Cicero finds the sphere-and-cylinder figure on a tombstone.

Shreds of its past wealth.
Five tons of gold for Venice alone.
Byzantium, snatched from Christendom, still its most glittering jewel.

But by then Archimedes's computations, people say, had squared the year.

THE STRANGER AT THE GATES

I thought:

The Method, so happily recovered.
I am the one who called us all together.
I driven time.
I wars and waves.
I was.
I go over sea-lanes rife with fish.
I did not.

I saw a shadow on the water.
I know this situation makes a perfect poem,
but I will not.
I want to write that I've already been to Jupiter,
but I have not,
or that Catholicism died in the darkness
of the already dark ages.

I a man mountain, a level island.
I a side-road.
I a dead toad on the side-road,
can only say what I've seen with my own eyes.
The heart inside us shakes
aswirl with evil.

I the eye in the wading pool
bathed in shame.
I sing for our time too.
I planned to follow all the "I's"
I could find.
I ahaze.
Not even the geese could make their way.
I sit down on the curb and wait.

Listen.
I loved him.

Our hour sat and sulked
but I a second hand
did not budge.
I an automobile.
I a blast furnace ensnared.
I a home like all the others in my neighborhood.
I at some other century
imaginary love affair
with heifers and others
left like a stranded hair.

I told you
I'd tell your story
if you just let me tell it.
I an embellishment
before the roads of the world grew dark.

I a moon making its way round.
I hate a metaphor.
I pissed on the sidewalk.
I did not.
I heard her heartbeat fifteen times
before she was born.
I a final glow of antiquity.
I "a method of exhaustion."
I felt her bare foot from the inside.
I streak the administration.
I bare myself too,
my breast to the moon
making its way round.

I resent you
whom I serve.
I said I would say
what you want
but say it my way.
I a television, a television.
I a giant model heart
touring the city-state

before slaves
in the birthplace
the cradle, etc.
I a swallow in your sight
loosed the sack and all the winds blew past.

I doled out my time
and money.
I was broke before
the reformation
the resurrection
and the restoration.

I a heathendom.
I a saintdom.
I a polka dot.
I cock-of-the-walk
cocksure, yelping
put beeswax in my ears.
I a dog in obedience class
who can no longer hear.

I say what you want me to say.
I say how brave.
I say how clever.
I say how we went together
happily.
How you loved me.
How we became a we
and I died and you lived on
restored and pretty.

BEATING OUT OF ITS SOMEWHERE PRINCELY BODY

The Method switches clothes with scarecrows.

Overlooking a broad, broad county fair in mid-Missouri,
muttering the words for wonder:

> Miracula   Mirus   Miror
> Mysterious lodestone
> Glowing carbuncle
> Petrifying springs

A tin man, escaped from Kansas,
wishes he had a heart.

Our mechanical friend buys two tickets for the merry-go-round.
Tin man, riding behind, rips this ticker from its horse,
title, deed, tombstone, coin, picture, etc.

PARCHMENT, PLEASE

Near the year
1000
we find
Maximos Planudes
nude
writing to a friend
in Asia Minor
asking for parchment
because the right quality
is not for sale
in his own neighborhood,
presumably Constantinople.

In the end,
all he receives
are some asses' skins,
which do not please
him in the least,
and a note:

Dear Max,

No parchment
till the summer,
months after the population
begins to eat meat.
Low yield
should come as no surprise,
our medieval animals
being much smaller
than their modern
counterparts.

Love,
A. Minor

THE METHOD RUBS ELBOWS WITH FRAT BOYZ

The neighborhood hums with anticipation.
Let us not forget, we live among the elderly.
Is it nothing to all ye who pass by
who pipe fuckn' flutes next door
among the stinking bottles
of last night's par-tee?

He hath hedged me about, better, walled me in 4-ever.
The popular sixth grade equation
slurred on my block:
so-and-so + so-and-so = true love.

And now, at 1:32 in the afternoon,
the Neanderthal boys fence with a cardboard box
& plastic machete on their scorched lawn
and now the girls cry in the hammocks
to find he has gone slinking down some alley
back to some second century, licking his chops.

AND YOU YOURSELF ARE A RESIDENT OF THIS CITY

Through the city, Method markes his way

> *Methinks mias-*
> *ma*
> *fallen in shrubs*
> *has left our city a series*
> *of suburbs*

By all means, be wary of ends
hankering for revenge
herded together
in our otherwise silent square.

In hospital, Middle-Aged men
exchange their hearts with ours.

I swear by this city
and by the begetter
and all whom he begot,
I'm the word of God.

> History is adorned
> With bookish fires.
>   —Geoffrey Hill, *Canaan*

                 ago into the blaze   we go we go

goosefooted   agog   over hardwood   & snow

No house troubled, no lawn hurt, I take the side

                        walks ways they go

various poxes then   appear

                maimed & mangled
                      on the body's marsh

         agone   ago ago   a
gaping
               hole   d
                  up

and hammering equations into gold   Method hefts a hearty

  heart

                   looks straight ahead

          saltwort
          ragwort

                alone   ablaze

     while the past
           preens itself
           at the pool's edge

His 99 most beautiful names lost

UNDER THE LEA OF THE SPANKER

This spring the angles were returned.
Sunlight somehow made its way back into the afternoon,
and through the pane of glass, rested on an angle,
refracting and shining onto Archimedes's sleeping forehead.

Archimedes took the Method to his knee
until his bottom half resembled a raging fire.

Roughly copied caricature, the Method thinks,
this injustice ought to make someone
somewhere stand up and do something
for something, he thinks.

He admired his sentence. Someone. Something. Somewhere.
How ambiguous can we make our enemy? How unclear can my call
    to action be?
Elevated only so slightly to red, the city stops. No one moves.

Turns out, the Method thinks, I'm not only angry, I'm ineffectual.

TRAP EASE

Weapons are just "geometry at play."
History fails to say
what decision he reached about the honesty of the goldsmith.

But I know other leaders who are wearing fake gold crowns.
"No Roman," Whitehead said, "would have lost his life because he was absorbed
in the contemplation of a mathematical equation."

You clumsy little numbering system, alphabet,
Look what you've done!
You've trapped yourself easily

in some auction house
some circus act
swinging eternally,
eating your own net.

THE NIGHTLY VISITANT

By heaven, and by the nightly visitant!
Would that you knew what the nightly visitant is.
It is the star of piercing brightness.

As the Method mulls this over, his bed coverings shift.
Someone slips in beside him, silently.
Someone sets a hand over his mouth, softly.
Someone lifts his teddy bear from his grip, gently.

At the Baltimore museum, the Method had met an exhibit of holy-
     mouthed men
set upon a bundle of hog hairs.
Had they tracked him here to bristle him in his bed, he asked Allah.

They scheme against you: but I too have My schemes.
Therefore, bear with the unbelievers, and let them be awhile.

_____ METHOD

The
(Thee)
(____)
Mr._____
Measly and/or Master_____
Archimedes's & a _____ & _____ &
my__

Tthe, the____

_____.

THE METHOD SOMEHOW SURVIVES
THE FOURTH CRUSADE

If there were wire-pullers at work,
the great artery of the city, Triumphal Way,
resembled a constellation:

rank and road   mud   oversea
                                                                     oversee
                        1800 ships
            crossbowmen   broadbeamed merchant men
ballistas

                        spear-hurling catapults
                        designed by a method-maker

    "a party of drunken Franks   set the mosque on fire"

bahariz (folk from the sea)   ate all eels in the river

                        leaving

    a grappled prow   an iron beak
                casks sunken in water

& crimson devices   he had "taken the cross"

            banners   fathom   only after

        "provisions for the host"   amass
                                                 mast

19

the Method
crouching in
his corner
hides,
rearranging his
organs, "heart
stay here," he
says, "but keep
ticking

but softly,"
he says.

WE EMBRACE THINGS WE CONSIDER UNHEARD OF

from his corner
the Method sees
the methods
of torture:

if there had been a hanging machine
or quartering
had there been the stake and wheel
the gallows
beating detainees with broom handles and chairs
military dogs
bed of nails
if there had been sodomizing with chemical lights
or steam machines
cat-o-nine-tails
if there was a network of gazes
a ball and chain
a scaffold
or photographs
of smiling guards
pointing to penises

(the other option was to take eastern Islam from the rear)

I take courage and flee,
carry it carefully
in my pants
& under my hat
spotted pards
sing a song

& it's like looking
at a noise
faraway, closer

TISCHENDORF TAKES A LEAF

The Method had heard some say:
"he or she
took a little part of me
when they took their leave
of me."

He had not understood
what was really meant:

> "Tearing one leaf from
> my others
> Constantine von Tischendorf
> carried off
> a little leaf of me"

the Method cried,

> "a little leaf of me Tishy-dwarf
> carried to Cambridge."

THE COMPLETE SENTENCE FOR MY FATHER

This is a complete sentence.
Does not frighten me.
The story of the dwarf,
confined forever,
to a complete sentence,
for his robbery, robby.
We must serve.
A complete sentence.
Otherwise.
If we do not.
Whose to say.
What a nice American Is.
Other than to say, wise.
Because my little god knows me
and he served
a complete sentence.
Winnow, what horses do,
that is winning, what we do
in the fields.
When we serve
what we wish to say, completely.
In the fields.
If we want the Method
to make a sentence
completely.
He must complete the fourth grade.
Otherwise.
He'll be left
behind. behead.
ed.
When we watch
the dwarf
take a page.
Completely from the Method.
If we say, Stop!
That is a complete

sentence. When we complete
something we feel good.
Completion is
a self-esteem booster.
All American children
should be completers.
Without completion,
we have no progress.
Without progress,
we have no completion.
The complete sentence
is lionized.
The fiercest beast
in the jungle.
In fact, no jungle
is complete.
Without one.
When we see one,
we halt.
we waltz.
I'm utterly.
I'm completely.
In love
with the sentence.
I will serve it
gladly.
You should
Serve it
completely.
Otherwise.

THE BOOK OF WORTHY CONQUEST

The Method recalls a miniature:
The yet-to-be-conquered Hungarian castle
in the distance.
An Ottoman vizier with a large plumed turban
sits under a decorated tent.
The commander of the castle,
hat in hand, humbly meets his Conqueror.
Could this be considered worthy?
A Method so thoroughly confused
checks his facts, and yes,
        the Ottomans assure him,
Yes.

Yes, hurlears

             a loon   hears

     a hunch   in some   sad   era

                                    of elocution

some centuries ago   alone   deft

the Method hurt
hurls his trumpet at a passing tree   an error

                and train rolls on and trail la-la's
        Allah's rails lost   ill laws

la la
how to be a hireling
                rather than on loan, on loan forever
                                              alone

                                        la

an era's law
showing the
sharpness of
its teeth

THE FUTURE OF AN ILLUSION

When one has lived for quite a long time in a particular civilization and has often tried to discover what its origins were and along what path it has developed, one sometimes also feels tempted to take a glance in the other direction and to ask what further fate lies before it and what transformations it is destined to undergo.

—Sigmund Freud

*

Perhaps I could use my own words just this once and make Method mouth what I desire. I desire God have his own destiny too, and that sometime, in the future, I might meet it on the road.

Waiting for the future is a failure we all perform. We thought to escape this by the work of the same civilization of which we ourselves are the enemy. Or, by those things known as miracles. But matter-of-factness matters.

We cannot just say somethings. Afterall, Chadwick's cancer returned. Erika is deaf in her right ear and Amy will have another Other. There is evidence that "Other" stretches back to around 1300 A.D.. Now it makes me sick to say; in fact, Other refers only back to me anyway. There is another other who is someone somewhere, and yet another who is a stranger and a suspect.

**

Illusions are not errors. Illusions are derived from human wishes. I wish the human would somehow make matter measure material, make Method march around the globe with flaglines & drumlines & horns & uniforms. In other words, parade around, creating an event. Existence is a wilderness of events, and I desire to get lost in that kind of thicket.

The future is full of heart transplants & face transplants. But I have a bungalow in which I lie low. Method miming me shows his palms and frowns. A baby with boar-like tusks turned away.

Discovering the philosophy of 'As if,' Method can't keep his mouth shut   now matter is all that matters. The illusion robbed of its future. Method tattles, and with Robin Hood dead on the road, he steals away.

> Cryst have mercy on his soule,
> That dyed on the rode!
> For he was a good outlawe,
> And dyde pore men moch god.

I'll ask the question no one wants me to ask: Method, who is the hero of this poem? Whose metropolis romps its pages? In the 4th century A.D., the Book appeared as parchment bound between wooden boards, and that's when evil, that little devil, made his rounds around the globe.

***

I remember the hotdog trees in Florida that fifth summer when we all went to Disneyworld. I remember the world before Disney, and it was the happiest place on earth.

The accident is a childhood memory we all share. The time we threw the boomerang and it didn't come back, slicing our friend's eye open. The time our sister fell off the monkey bars, or at least that is what we were instructed to tell our parents. The time we ran our go-cart into the ditch. The time we broke our leg on the teeter-totter because our brother jumped off suddenly. If there had been enough of these accidents, or if they had been serious enough, or if we had had less hospitals and McDonald's, perhaps there would be enough food to feed the other children.

As a pioneer, Method had to eat his relatives during a long winter lost in the mountains. When he came over the pass the following spring, he was overweight, and he longed to be an American. But by 2020 the French will be as fat as we are.

In many ways, the mountains were the happiest place on earth, for he could always see Orion, and he managed to keep his little dog alive by giving him the bones. No one was searching for him, stealing from him, translating him. In the mountains, he used his own pages to kindle the fire.

✳✳✳✳

There is no reason to return home, even though my home is now bigger than it once was, being a ranch with not a single cow or horse. Method realizes others must have the same thoughts, but their parents busily distribute missing person posters and their police scour the fields and rivers. Ultimately, there is no place like it, but saying it will not get you there.

It doesn't matter whether or not you like prose poems, because you are bound to like one or the other. "The proper METHOD for studying poetry and good letters is the method of contemporary biologists, that is careful first-hand examination of the matter, and continual COMPARISON of one 'slide' of specimen with another." A feeling of progress creeps in; the memory becomes a cord connecting us to this house, feeding us, and we recognize that we will probably die here.

✳✳✳✳✳

This much is unthinkable:

 "It is certain because it is impossible."

* * * * * *

When you enter some deceased stranger's house and see their belongings for sale, you either feel excited because you see something you like and can afford, or disgusted because whose to say how important that object was to them. After all, Method always thought he ought to fetch more than he did, and perhaps his anonymous owner is cursed because of it. That same year, Christie's price-fixing problems arose.

As the auctioneer explained, we use the term almost-common-values to mean (somewhat inconsistently) almost-pure-common-values. That the thoughts of many hearts may be revealed, a sword shall pierce thine own soul, I told him in response. That is when the thatches caught fire and nearly consumed me.

If only we could join the Secret Kingdom of the Swifts where our belongings would be hidden behind the Kaieteur Falls in the heart of Guyana. On the one hand, we'd give ourselves over to the downdraft, while on the other, we'd be strong enough not to plunge into the river below. I desire to squat in their cave behind the falls, but I am an employee and am expected at work.

* * * * * * *

I proceed as a companion, but eventually I will be told to wait outside. A stranger in the house I built. Sparrows circle my head and squirrels and rabbits accompany me into the wilderness. At some point this spring, I will be shot. It is just like an animal to frolic heartily in the face of such danger. These are our imaginings of animal life, and even when we allow them into our homes, we don't completely understand why. Perhaps subconsciously we are looking for some magic formula that will turn children into creative adults. And now that I will have my own, I will try as well. After all, we only want the best for *our* children.

The ongoingness originally fascinated me, which is why I became a follower. How someone collects interest as I breathe. How someone survives inside because I choose to eat. How Method will long outlive me, his rottenness all cleaned up and smelling pretty. I hope someone unearths me and puts his nose to my eyeholes. If we believe that "people follow the paths of migrating birds, beautiful strangers, and lost manuscripts trying to keep the things sensorily present to them," then we have followed only tangentially. But then, I am sure of an afterlife, a collection of the most distant sideroads lined with flowers and poison oak, and at least my Method will be excluded from somewhere.

****

We learn the most important things first, in grade school: If I walk ahead and appear as though I don't care to be included, to be invited in, to have a place at the table, I will be desired. "All writing is a demonstration of method; it can assume a method or investigate it." But can it do both at once? I assume my place at the table, then I vacate it, then I investigate it. Imaginary friends attended the first tea party I ever hosted, and those same friends will most likely attend the last, at which point I will learn the most important things:

"my wife   my car   my color   and   myself."

Autumn is now ancient history. We've raked the leaves, dragged the lawn furniture into the garage, and ploughed the garden. By this time, the illusion is dismantling itself, and the only place to go is the museum. I separate myself from Method, or he separates himself from me, leaving behind only a sheet of substance and a trampoline. If I jump high enough, I see over the sheet, but he ducks and taunts me. Next time I get my hands on him, I will

****

Method wants a luxury vacation, a Caribbean cruise or three weeks in Hawaii. He wants buckets, beach balls, shovels and suntan lotion. The false lure of leisure time. But the truth is, we do not know what the jellyfish feels as it stings us. From his beach blanket, he sees great distances of lives, a mass of withering lintels & wattles & lemmings. Luckily, the tide rises and pulls it all under. He rolls over, sunning his other side.

Later he'll stroll the boardwalk, vamping the once lively amusement park rides with paper clips and safety pins. If only he had a metal detector, he could find a past buried in the soft sand. Method is beginning to believe that the ocean, with all of its hurricanes and tsunamis, has its own desires for a landlocked holiday.

Imagine, after all this time, we are only on a river in the middle of South America where the dolphins deceive us. How happy they are, deceived themselves, to be on the other side. You've always feared drowning, haven't you? You've always wondered if you'd take that last gasp knowing it was not air. Well, you would. Considering all we've been through, I'd still hurl Master Method into the ocean if we were ever to reach its shores.

****

Method had his fortune "read" by a rabbit outside the Blue Mosque. *Looking for satisfaction in far away places will not lead you there.* We were unable to assess the authenticity of the fortuneteller since what was predicted had already happened. Like the objects our dog drags out from under the deck: first, a tin lid, and days later, its can. After months in his weather pattern, we finally lose him, citing "when in the course of human events" as reason enough to go on without him.

We had ties to Turkey, but it had its way with us before we arrived. The country was locked and we needed permits we didn't have. I would have said, "I am a poet writing a book," but Nina was certain this would be of little consequence. Gordon climbed over piles of discarded wrappers and lottery tickets, old mattresses and broken bottles; he scaled the graffitied walls at St. John Studios to take the photos I needed for my "research." Love like a tin lid, and later on, its can. Now you recognize me, limping alongside what we call "persona.". A mammoth hole in the manuscript was filled with stones so that even if we were to happen upon him again, we'd be unable to lift him.

****

Everyone insists that I will write about pregnancy, but I won't. For one embarrassing second, I thought I would quit the project altogether. Someone calls her a "passenger," another a "hijacker." I will, however, write about my own birth. The doctor arrived bloody. After a night of heavy drinking, he had walked through a sliding glass door. Think of method as an infant—he was born with a full head of black hair. At this very moment, the scientists are transplanting hair follicles, and soon he will look like his "old self" again.

I adopt a new-old method: "Up to this point I have confined what I have written to the results of my own direct observation and research, and the views I have formed from them; but from now on the basis of my story will be the accounts given to me by the Egyptians themselves— though here, too, I shall put in one or two things which I have seen with my own eyes." But the question of "voice" remains because 1. you can't call this silence and 2. you can't call silence. It won't budge.

****

Happening or not, we wait in the areaway.

****

Whose responsibility is it to make sure we all have jobs? Someone must do the dirty work, the hard work, the boring work. Method wants to rearrange the facts to ward off this ordinariness. He never worked a day in his life, and this someone will eventually take revenge. As the worker walks home from the lumberyard, he spots Method swaying in a hammock and slaughters him. And who's to say he doesn't have the right? Poetry can hardly be called "an honest days work." But let's remember, it doesn't pay either.

Most of us have had jobs we couldn't bear: assembling glove compartments, cleaning cheap rooms in hotel-casinos, washing dishes at the A&W, landscaping planned communities. But what did we buy with our wages? Beer, gas, clothing, and books. As we grow older, fresh "problems" emerge: Would it have been better to get one of those new houses in the suburbs where someone else's mistakes don't appear to be your own? He speculates: decades ago a previous drunk owner must have thought it a good idea to have another beer and paint the trim. I propose: he wasn't drunk but old and shaky, trying his best to improve what will years later become *our* house.

* * * * * * * * * * * *

In the distance, I hear America swimming. It is a hot day, and we are circling the island. They find his inflatable crocodile humorous, and they point and chuckle among themselves. Method began to keep track of such embarrassments by writing a Souda, a compilation of compilations. In it he includes etymological ponderings, such as the relationship between "moor," to secure a ship, and the Moors. A ship is moored when she rides by two anchors. *Mooring chains and Morning chains*, he chants softly as he floats.

* * * * * * * * * * * * *

I made this florilegium for you, you know, and now we have things to put back in order before we finish. There are the vacancies to fill in the foothills. The trees are gone, so up go the houses. That's either the direct road or an oasis that shines in the distance.

It eventually resembles a dump, something unsightly and sickly, teetering drunkenly on the precipice. The stench rises up, and when the wind blows in the proper direction, you can smell everyone else's rejections. Yet in my dream, the audience keeps screaming, "more, more, encore, encore." Method knows better. The temporary illusion of success brought on by the dream, and the subsequent realization of failure made it harder than usual to work today. Still, I need a souvenir to prove I went along for the pointless highway ride. Next time I suggest taking only inroads.

I eventually realize it is not heart one hungers after, though we like to say, "so-and-so has heart." It is desire, and without it we'd be happy, finally. At this late hour, Method moans a little with sleepiness. But when the future presents itself, we duck and run—it is scary enough without its past attached.

SOURCES

✷✷A *Gest of Robyn Hode, The Eighth Fytte*
✷✷✷✷ Ezra Pound, *ABC of Reading*
✷✷✷✷✷ Tertullian, *De Carne Christi*
✷✷✷✷✷✷✷ Elaine Scarry, *On Beauty and Being Just*
✷✷✷✷✷✷✷✷ Charles Bernstein, *Content's Dream*; Charles Olson, *Maximus Poems*
✷✷✷✷✷✷✷✷✷✷ Herodotus, *The Histories*

A TWILIGHT WORLD OF CONSENT
RATHER THAN BELIEF

mr. method moves sheepishly
through the dump
muttering,
method must,
method must be an encyclopediaist
a cyclist

moving over mounds of rubbish
this once was a bottom bracket axle,
a crank, a shifter, a pedal
a mending machine
a duty to believe
an impossible
collection
of objects and ideas
migrated here
simply to become
a sequential history

method muttering, *what strange abundance and even stranger shortages.*

THE SAND RECKONER

Archimedes showed how sand could be counted. Certainly one can find
out how many grains of sand would equal the diameter of a poppy seed,
he said, and from that one can proceed to work out how many poppy
seeds would equal the width of a finger and then the arms of a half moon.

This is how marvels became vulgar,
how we came to sneer at the passing vagabond.
The man had the figure of a sphere-and-cylinder engraved on his
tombstone,
for Christ's sake. It is a wonder we wondered after this.

10^{63} poppy seeds fill the universe

THE PROPERTY OF A DECEASED'S ESTATE

No more auction block for me No more bitter block.

No more bidder's call for me No more winner's curse.

No more peck o'corn for me No more pint o' salt.

No more driver's lash for me No more master's call.

No more buyer a or b seller c or d

nor lock & key.

No more auction block. Me & many

                       thousands gone.

ME THEE ODES

Method's wealth is went away
his twelfth time down to the bar.
He's on the outs. He stinks.
He has his way with me.
He is some sad
sulking.

He is not these things.
He is not.

He sats all day poking out.
He rots, and riles his heart.
He moves underground.
He bucks me off.
He hangs around, loiters
gives up for lent
the following:

He carries a bell for bears,
to scare them off.
He's tender towards me.
I sell him down the river,
all shitty and sorry.

He's bigger than me.
He's better.
He's all round and his rump
is lovely.

He went again
to the bar and lost
his thirteenth.

And shot a dart through
the window
hitting all but me.

He is his own he.
He is.
His is dead and gone,
and his comes along,
very scary. Boo
hoo.

His is one too many.

He is an object that looks like an object.
I love an object that looks like an object.
He is an object that looks like an object.
He is not.

He fell
a forest
over
and so broke
his crown

A body without a head
is no more to be feared

than a land without
a king, he said.

He is himself about the ground,
rolling and wild
with his
own
heart
pounding

and full of piss and fire
God Bless him
and his.

Method is his own his
And no one else's.

He looks like him and his,
anyway,
he eats like him and his
and so he is.

CHRISTIE'S AUCTION HOUSE
since 1766

36-year-old midshipman becomes an auctioneer.
In his Pall Mall garden salesroom, he sold fog to Londoners,
several bales of hay, 62 million *Sunflowers*, me
                                        and Thackeray:

> "I have just come from a dismal sight—full of snobs looking
> at furniture. Foul people: odious bombazine women; brutes
> keeping their hats on in the kind old drawing-room. I longed
> to knock some of them off, and say, Sir, be civil in a lady's
> room!' Ah, it was a strange, sad picture of Vanity Fair!"

A silk Tabriz Persian Prayer Rug (butter-colored), late 19th century,
the property of a European Lady. $6,000-$8,000.

A Greek Corinthian-type Bronze Helmet, circa early 5th century b.c.
Of hammered steel, neckguard flaring, cheek-pieces each half-spade
shaped, a slightly raised ridge outlining the perimeter of the helmet.
$60,000-$80,000.

A pair of mulitgem and gold black moor broaches. Comprising two
carved blackamoors, one wearing a rose and circular cut ruby turban,
the other wearing a vari-cut emerald helmet with a ruby tunic.
$4,000-$6,000.

Lot and His Daughters. A fan painted with Lot's wife becoming a
pillar of salt, the ivory sticks carved and pierced with figures, baskets,
and flowers. (one stick repaired) $1,900-$2,800.

[Civil War] Lee, Robert E. Autograph Letter to Brigadier General
J.E.B. Stuart, Headquarters. 18 August, 1862. Marked Confidential:

> "I hope to be prepared today
> to cross tomorrow."
> $30,000-$40,000.

METHOD MEETS YOUNG LOVE AMONG THE ROFES

"dear is my little native vale"
"dear is my two on the banks"
"dear is my tank in a field"
"dear is my friendly dog, O"
"dear is my eel in a bowl"
"dear is my stew in the pot"
"dear is my god on a cloud"
"dear is my tree by the road"
"dear is my ghost in a bed"
"dear is my bird in the bush"
"dear is my hand on a rod"
"dear is my love
                among the rofes."

KAYMAKAMLAR GEZI EVI, SELAMLIK ODASI

This is the room.
Where mole guests are welcomed.
At this moment you see the wedding table prepared for the mole guests.

Rooms are heated with stoves.
Rooms have been designed according to the patriarchal way of living.
The family has, consists of, father, mather, sons and brides.
There is no sex discrimination within the family.
They artogether, have meal and altogether chat, but when the doors
    are clased.

Mole guests are welcomed in "Selamlik" part.
Femole guests are welcomed in "Harem" part.
On such occasions mole guests are served via the cupboard in the wall
    which turns on its axis.

METHOD INTERVIEWS A MONK

Was Christianity given to man by God from the beginning?
No, God acts like a schoolmaster.

How could you prove the origin of Christianity is divine?
A tree is known by its fruits.

Does God provide for the world He created?
If a hut is left neglected for a little while, it becomes a ruin.

How does the conscience work?
When we are going to perform any act, the conscience, if our act agrees
with the will of God, persistently and imperatively orders us to proceed to
the act.

Describe a Church to me.
A church is always a large and imposing building proclaiming the piety
of the congregation, and so built that those who pray in it shall look
Eastward; for the natural sun was always considered as an emblem of "the
Father of lights."

What tools are used for the Liturgy of the Catechumens?
The asterisk and the disc, the spoon, the spear, the oblation.

OUR OWN DAZZLING VARIETY OF SECTS

Surely the people is grass   light rather than line lies at the heart of the field
and beyond   the Shaker village   a network of surprising
asymmetry

Swallowtailed   Less Figural

The textual woof and wefts   threads
that precede words   teetering on the Leap Day
when Ann Lee was born   a quiet fanatic hiding behind

dashes   dots   triangles   small   arcs
the underside   of a leaf

had she said   *a size you can walk into*
we would have entered

but there is no straight line   between belief and building

I was embraced by that object   I behaved
I was enthusiastick   I was a tree   each branch embroidered with fire
I was a calm of regulation   and restraint

but I no longer believed belief was too busy
to worry   about composition

it's just that what we see   changes as we grow more distant

everything in the Shaker world,   laid out in rows, grids
rejects the human body   as a primary form

claw feet and pedestals   with delicate objects atop
merely   a kag of apple sass

fine   .   but nonexistent
their "visionary drawings" lulled

lost   among the gewgaw
or perhaps hidden   in an off-centered drawer
in their perfect cabinets

PALINODE

> O dove, fly to Aleppo with my Byzantine ode
> And take my greeting to my kinsman.
> —Mahmoud Darwish

Before I was born, I saw a tissue of ingenious detours, an inextricable tangle
wreathed with mistake.

Perhaps the ghost does not limp away, but rather forests flee me, frightened.
Look, they are setting a place for loss, clearing the table for the first glow of
antiquity.

Here we see William T. Walters in his little library illuminated, carefully
smoothing the lip of the continent.

What form bounds forward from behind but The Atlantic Railroad Coastline Co.?
The whole Roman Empire was sold by ascending auction in 193 A.D.

A globe enclosed. Bottomless years. The train has stopped on the platform and no
one is there, for these are the Public Days, when the "Poor Association" claims the
museum's building.

As if bound by the knots of invention, I found a wrong road dotted with weeds
and sorrows.

A SECOND OFFENCE FOR JOHN BERRYMAN

If you had never seen a second snow
in Baltimore or Minneapolis, what matter, really
marveled Method,
scratching himself slowly in solemn spots.
You joined thought with thought though outwent
measly Method to live on

rotten and stinking up the world's libraries.
O joyous departures fumbling in the trees,
coming emptily.
It wasn't the thought they thought they could
do it, was it,
out with it:

what was it, then, got under your pelt?
As you say, we suffer on, a day, a day, a day.
The weather's bad,
the sun much worse, yet Method jogs,
pays bills, banters buddies, winks, shits, and sleeps
while your ghost limps comelier away.

UNMAKING, MAKING

River,
      River,
River,
       cross me.
Come on, our house is ready.
We've hoarded, we've cleaned,
we've packed our bags with pain and imagining.

Method wonders, what womb made me?
He climbs his family tree,
yells down:

    Take courage, the buzzards flew away,
    the bluebirds await.

PANTOUM

Perhaps the universe is an extinguished building
with blue banners strung along
and the forest, more like a commodity
bordering bushes and asphalt,

something else to string our blue banners on.
Never was restoration swifter:
the leafless trees, the asphalt
less splintered and more splendid.

Never was restoration swifter
with its mightier solutions,
less splintered and more splendid
snipers, dynamiters, colorful bombs.

We please ourselves with mightier solutions,
picnics under blue spruces
snipers, dynamiters, colorful bombs
the guardians of what we might call "home rights."

At picnics, under blue spruces
we clamor after the news
and its employees, the guardians of "home rights"
"the media" mustering "one mind."

It's news,
the decision to nobly save rather than meanly lose
some pretense of mustering "one mind"
secures its truth.

The decision to nobly save rather than meanly lose
our flag
secures its truth
as a squirrel secures its nuts by hiding them in the ground.

Our flag—
a souvenir of having been here before
a squirrel's nuts, deep in the ground.
but travel, travail, and The Method's mistakes

all souvenirs of having been here before,
haunt us and taunt us and call us names.
But travail, travel, and Method's mistakes
mark a different season, nuts rotting, bulbs blooming.

Each season haunts us and taunts us and calls us names
until finally the universe is an extinguished building,
a different season, nuts rotting, bulbs blooming
and the forest, a commodity.

WEST EATS MEAT

Master Method emerges on the street
                              snout & cleft feet

he hogs the grazing land
and we go hungry,
not even an oint-
-ment left in the bowl

until
run over
by a hummer,
            he's matted, flattened, worn, warn.

Our hour has arrived,
a platter garnished with roast feet.
We eat.

No wonder,
ourselves and our monsters on parade
& on stage, an olive tree leaved with sparrows sings:

            "a worm a worm
                eats word
                eastward
                east's warned"

IN PALESTINE

Its hard to hate a people,
Method chants,

Saba, Savva,
old man,
fiih,

when you've read
their poetry.

IF THERE WERE A LEVER LARGE ENOUGH AND ANOTHER WORLD, HE WOULD MOVE THIS ONE

In the field-furrow
the rainwater

evaporates
and stems

retreat
into the ground.

Where a Turk
plants his feet,

Method was told,
grass never grows

a   gain
on our side

we have the Judean desert
and forty days & nights

for Christ to wander
and finally

after descending
into the ravine bed

the Kidron passes
to the Dead Sea

the foot of Mar Saba
Mar Savva

1500 years of continuous prayer
perched on a mountain

rising in stories and terraces
a series of antechambers

a pile of hermit skulls
left behind.

Method climbs a ladder,
creeps through a small door

into the scriptorium.
St. Saba, healer monk,

loved my later layer,
Method recalls,

with all its exorcisms
for unclean spirits

and prayers for the sick
in a desert fought over

by ancient, some say, inhabitants
and desperate children.

Looking over the landscape,
your level levels

a field
all   ready

void of grass.
Let me level with you,

gangs of hoarfrost
brought light to my pocket

and fire to my home.

THIS PLAIN PLACE

Nothing has happened in this place
and it happened forever
until recently.
It was forever happening
amid Method's fluctuating vision.
He heard rustling in the bushes,
the bandicoot poking around in its pouch,
to pull finally nothing
out.

He understood the animal's sorrow
to find plainly and without denial
emptiness where a relation ought to be
a deep and majestic blue
into which one carefully
places
a heart,
plainly
steps back,
places
a body around
a heart,
steps back
into a past place where
only the monks,
deathly afraid of nothing,
turn the deaf
away.

Fence Books is an extension of *Fence;* a biannual journal of poetry, fiction, art, and criticism that has a mission to redefine the terms of accessibility by publishing challenging writing distinguished by idiosyncrasy and intelligence rather than by allegiance with camps, schools, or cliques. It is part of our press's mission to support writers who might otherwise have difficulty being recognized because their work doesn't answer to either the mainstream or to recognizable modes of experimentation.

The Motherwell Prize (formerly the Alberta Prize) is an annual series that offers publication of a first or second book of poems by a woman, as well as a one thousand dollar cash prize.

Our second prize series is the Fence Modern Poets Series. This contest is open to poets of any gender and at any stage of career, and offers a one thousand dollar cash prize in addition to book publication.

For more information about either prize, visit www.fenceportal.org, or send an SASE to: Fence Books/[Name of Prize], New Library 320, University at Albany, 1400 Washington Avenue, Albany, NY, 12222.

For more about *Fence,* visit www.fenceportal.org.

Fence Books

THE MOTHERWELL PRIZE

Aim Straight at the Fountain and Press Vaporize	Elizabeth Marie Young
Unspoiled Air	Kaisa Ullsvik Miller

THE ALBERTA PRIZE

The Cow	Ariana Reines
Practice, Restraint	Laura Sims
A Magic Book	Sasha Steensen
Sky Girl	Rosemary Griggs
The Real Moon of Poetry and Other Poems	Tina Brown Celona
Zirconia	Chelsey Minnis

FENCE MODERN POETS SERIES

Star in the Eye	James Shea
Structure of the Embryonic Rat Brain	Christopher Janke
The Stupefying Flashbulbs	Daniel Brenner
Povel	Geraldine Kim
The Opening Question	Prageeta Sharma
Apprehend	Elizabeth Robinson
The Red Bird	Joyelle McSweeney

NATIONAL POETRY SERIES

Collapsible Poetics Theater	Rodrigo Toscano

ANTHOLOGIES & CRITICAL WORKS

*Not for Mothers Only: Contemporary Poets on Child-Getting &
Child-Rearing*   Catherine Wagner & Rebecca Wolff, editors

POETRY

The Method	Sasha Steensen
The Orphan & Its Relations	Elizabeth Robinson
Site Acquisition	Brian Young
Rogue Hemlocks	Carl Martin
19 Names for Our Band	Jibade Khalil Huffman
Infamous Landscapes	Prageeta Sharma
Bad Bad	Chelsey Minnis
Snip Snip!	Tina Brown Celona
Yes, Master	Michael Earl Craig
Swallows	Martin Corless-Smith
Folding Ruler Star	Aaron Kunin
The Commandrine & Other Poems	Joyelle McSweeney
Macular Hole	Catherine Wagner
Nota	Martin Corless-Smith
Father of Noise	Anthony McCann
Can You Relax in My House	Michael Earl Craig
Miss America	Catherine Wagner

FICTION

Flet: A Novel	Joyelle McSweeney
The Mandarin	Aaron Kunin